BASIC LESSONS FOR PARLIMENTARY PROCEDURE INSTRUCTION
THIRD EDITION

A Hobar Publications Workbook

First Globe Pequot edition 2019

All rights reserved.
No part of this book may be reproduced in any form or by any electronic or mechanical means, including information storage and retrieval systems, without written permission from the publisher, except by a reviewer who may quote passages in a review.

Published by Hobar Publications
An imprint of Globe Pequot Press
Wholly Owned by: The Rowman & Littlefield Publishing Group, Inc.
4501 Forbes Boulevard, Suite 200
Lanham, Maryland 20706

Distributed by National Book Network
1-800-462-6420

INTRODUCTION

These materials, lesson plans and overhead masters are designed to assist instructors who teach a course or series of units dealing with parliamentary procedure.

An attempt has been made to follow the generally accepted rules of parliamentary law, Robert's Rules of Order, in compiling these lessons. Items that are infrequently used and items which are unique to special situations have not been included.

The author desires that every member of an organization knows how to participate in a meeting, conduct a meeting, and protect the rights of minorities, while seeing to it that the rights of the majority prevail. The author believes these goals may be accomplished through the use and study of the basic explanation of parliamentary law. When all group members can apply basic parliamentary laws, business can be conducted effectively and efficiently.

While learning activities have not been specified in the lessons, each student should demonstrate the ability to make each motion. Experience in presenting this material to agricultural education majors at the University of Minnesota has proven that when each class member not only makes the motion, but also assumes the chair and handles each motion, the rate of learning increases tremendously. The author recommends that the practice group(s) contain six to eight members and that students with competence in parliamentary procedure assist when more than one group is needed. It is desirable to prepare sets of subjects (topics) of interest to the students and abilities (motions) to be handled relative to this motion. For example:

Subject	Abilities
1. Fruit Sales	Main Motion Amend
2. Homecoming Dance	Main Motion Refer to Committee Amend

If these lessons are used to form the basis for a particular unit or course, at least 20 hours of contact time should be allocated. Where course structure allows, a series of time blocks should be used to maintain interest and to take advantage of the review process that occurs as students practice more complex parliamentary skills. For example, lessons 1 through 5 could be taught to ninth grade students and lessons 6 through 9 could be taught to tenth grade students or the lesson could be taught in nine two hour blocks on two week intervals during a given semester. Generally speaking, the complexity of the motions increases as one moves through the lessons 1 through 9.

LESSON 1

COURSE:

UNIT: Leadership

PROBLEM AREA: Parliamentary Procedure

PROBLEM: What are the essential features we must understand to interpret parliamentary procedure?

OUTCOMES:
1. Define parliamentary procedure.
2. List the order of business during a meeting.
3. Describe the different types of votes.
4. Describe the proper use of the gavel in a meeting.
5. Define precedence.

REFERENCE: Robert's Rules of Order

Key Question #1

What are the purposes of parliamentary procedure?

a. To transact business in an orderly manner.
b. To allow the will of the majority to rule, while protecting the rights of the minority.
c. To insure democracy in practice.
d. To guide members so they know when to expect items of business in a meeting.

Key Question #2

What is the established order of business to follow at meetings?

a. Minutes of the previous meeting.
b. Officer reports (including treasurer's report).
c. Committee reports.
   1. Standing (program of activities, etc.)
   2. Special (appointed at previous meetings)
d. Special features (speakers, special music) (This time it is optional.)
e. Unfinished business.
f. New business.
g. Adjournment.

If you have a special speaker on an item of business it may be courteous to change the order of business so that the presentation may be completed earlier in the program. Generally, this can be inserted before the unfinished business.

Key Question #3

What is the procedure for presenting the minutes of the previous meeting?

    a. Presiding officer requests Secretary's report.

    b. Secretary stands and reads the report.

    c. President asks for any additions or corrections.

    d. President then approves as read or approves as corrected, signifying the decision with one tap of the gavel. The tap of the gavel is optional and dependent on tradition or local bylaw specification.

Key Question #4

What should be included in the minutes of the meeting?

    a. Kind of meeting, whether it is a regular, annual, special, etc.

    b. The name of the organization.

    c. Date, time, and place of meeting.

    d. Notation of the presence of the regular presiding officer with his name and that of the secretary, if desired, or in their absence, the names of their substitutes.

    e. Whether the minutes of the previous meeting were read and approved.

    f. Receipts, disbursements, and balance in the treasury.

    g. Mention of important letters read by the secretary.

    h. Reports of committees (standing and special).

    i. All motions and disposition of each. All points of order and appeals, whether sustained or lost.

    j. Type of entertainment, refreshments, and special features at chapter meeting.

Key Question #5

What is the procedure for presenting the Treasurer's report?

    a. Presiding officer requests report.

    b. Treasurer stands and reads the report.

    c. Chair asks for any questions.

    d. Chair files subject to audit, signifying the decision with one tap of the gavel. The tap of the gavel is optional and dependent on tradition or local bylaw specification.

Key Question #6

What should be included in the Treasurer's report?

    a. Receipts:

Balance on hand at date of last report	$_____
Receipts (either total or itemized) since last report	$_____
Total receipts	$_____

    b. Disbursements:

Expenses (to whom and how much)	$_____
Total disbursements	$_____

    c. Present Balance $_____

Key Question #7

How should the gavel be used in the meeting?

The gavel should not be used as a device with which to make noise; it is the symbol of order and authority.

    a. One tap of the gavel can mean three things.
        1. Be seated.
        2. The motion passed or failed -- action is completed.*
        3. Follows announcements of reports.*

    b. Two taps of the gavel can mean only one thing.
        1. The meeting is called to order.

    c. Three taps of the gavel can mean only one thing.
        1. All members are to stand.

*Not used in all forms of meetings.

Key Question #8

What are the different types of votes that can be taken?

    a. Majority - more than half the total votes cast.

    b. Plurality - the largest number of votes received by a candidate when at least three choices are available, but is not necessarily a majority vote.

    c. Two-thirds - 2/3 of the votes cast. In determining if you have a 2/3 vote, double the negative vote and if the sum is greater than the affirmative vote, a 2/3 vote has not been obtained. Example:

        6 yes votes   8>6, therefore;
        4 no votes $4 + 4 = 8$ a 2/3s vote has not
        10 total votes   been obtained

Key Question #9

What are the different means by which to take a vote?

    a. A majority vote can be taken by voice, ballot, raising of hands, standing, or roll call.

    b. A 2/3 vote can be taken by ballot, raising of hands, standing, or roll call.

    c. Other less common means of voting are: mail ballot, absentee ballot, proxy, and general consent.

Key Question #10

What is meant by the term "precedence"?

Precedence is the order in which motions or items rank, it is the order in which they will be considered. Within parliamentary procedure each motion has a definite rank or order in which it can be legally handled. Because precedence or rank does not indicate the importance of a motion, it is possible to have several motions pending at the same time. Highest ranking motions are at the top of the list. While any motion is pending (not disposed of) the motions above are in order and the ones below are out of order.

Key Question #11

What are the different classifications of motions?

There are five general classes of motions. Three of those classes -- <u>main</u>, <u>subsidiary</u>, and <u>privileged</u> have a fixed order or precedence and are termed ordinary motions. The fourth class, <u>incidental</u> motions, has no order of precedence among themselves; they are applied to main and subsidiary motions. <u>Restoratory</u> motions, sometimes referred to as unclassified motions, are used to change something previously acted on at a meeting.

OH 1-1

TYPES OF VOTES

1) MAJORITY

2) PLURALITY

3) TWO-THIRDS

METHODS OF COUNTING VOTES

1) VOICE

2) BALLOT

3) RAISING HANDS

4) STANDING

5) ROLL CALL

6) VOTING BY MAIL

7) ABSENTEE BALLOT

8) PROXY

9) GENERAL OR UNANIMOUS CONTEST

PRECEDENCE

-- ORDER IN WHICH MOTIONS OR ITEMS RANK, IT IS THE ORDER IN WHICH THEY CAN BE CONSIDERED.

CLASSIFICATIONS OF MOTIONS

-- MAIN

-- SUBSIDIARY - RELATED TO THE PENDING MOTION

-- INCIDENTAL - INCIDENTAL TO THE PENDING MOTION, DEAL WITH FIRST

-- PRIVILEGED - NOT RELATED TO THE PENDING MOTION

-- RESTORATORY (UNCLASSIFIED)

LESSON 2

COURSE:

UNIT: Leadership

PROBLEM AREA: Parliamentary Procedure

PROBLEM: What procedure should we follow in obtaining the floor and in making and disposing of a main motion?

OUTCOMES:
1. To define a main motion.
2. To list the steps in obtaining the floor and making a main motion in its proper form.
3. To properly dispose of a main motion.

REFERENCES: Robert's Rules of Order
A Guide to Parliamentary Procedure - Melvin Henderson
The How in Parliamentary Procedure - Kenneth Lee Russell
The Meeting Will Come to Order - Harold Sponberg
Demeter's Manual of Parliamentary Procedure

Key Question #1

What is the purpose of the main motion?

> Other than a resolution, the main motion is the only means by which new business can be introduced to a group or meeting. It should be complete, but yet as direct as possible. An example of a main motion is: **"I move that we donate $50.00 to the Courage Foundation."**

Key Question #2

What is meant by the term floor?

> The term floor, as used in parliamentary procedure, means the exclusive right to be heard.

Key Question #3

What procedure should be followed in obtaining the floor, making the <u>main motion</u>, discussing, and voting on it?

Steps		Key Points
a. Rise and address the chair.	a.1	When no one has the floor, rise and say, **"Mr./Madam President."**
	a.2	State the chair's proper title: **"Mr. President," "Madam President,"** etc.
b. Gain recognition from the chair.	b.1	After you have addressed the chair, the President will recognize you by calling your name, nodding, pointing...
	b.2	In a large delegate body you may be asked to identify yourself so that people know who the motion is coming from.
c. Make the main motion.	c.1	State it in the form of **"I move that..."**
	c.2	**"I make a motion," "I wish to make a motion,"** or **"I so move"** are all <u>incorrect</u> statements.
d. Second the motion. (Cannot be seconded by the mover of the motion.)	d.1	State **"Mr./Madam President, I second the motion."**
	d.2	or **"Second"**,
	d.3	or **"I second the motion."**
	d.4	There is no need to be recognized when seconding a motion.
	d.5	In most instances, if there is no second heard, the chair will say, **"The motion is lost for want of a second."**
e. Statement of the motion.	e.1	After the motion is made and seconded, the chair restates it and its essential descriptive characteristics: whether it is amendable, debatable and the type or vote required.
	e.2	Once the chair restates the motion, it is then the property and business of the group. The motion is often called the pending question.
f. Gain recognition from chair for debate.	f.1	Priority is given to the mover of the motion.
	f.2	First person to address the chair.
	f.3	Member who has not yet spoken is given priority over one who has already spoken.
	f.4	Discussion should be alternated between pro and con people of the issue if possible.

		f.5 No person has the right to speak more than twice on an issue if another person who wishes to speak has not yet spoken.
g.	Putting the question.	g.1 The chair restates the motion after it is evident there is no further discussion.
h.	Voting on the motion.	h.1 A main motion requires a majority vote, usually a voice vote is sufficient.
		h.2 In the case of the presiding officer being unable to decide, he can call for a hand vote (division of the assembly).
i.	Ruling on the vote.	i.1 Presiding officer must call the motion passed or failed.
		i.2 Presiding officer should indicate the effect of the passage or failure.
		i.3 Seal passage or failure with one tap of gavel.

Key Question #4

What is a resolution?

A resolution is simply a main motion which is submitted in writing and in a more formal manner. Several reasons may be given in a preamble with the terminology of **Whereas** being used. The intent is then stated after the term **Resolved**. After the intent is stated, the person will say, **"I move the adoption of this resolution."**

Example:

"**Whereas, the Rapid Park FFA Chapter has had success in raising pheasants;**

Whereas, the Rapid Park Chapter of the Future Farmers of America has received much monetary support for its Pheasant Release Program from the Rapid Park Market Company; and

Whereas, Mr. Roy Johnson of Rapid Park Market Company has been responsible for the procurement of this monetary support; therefore be it

Resolved, that Mr. Roy Johnson be installed as an honorary member of the Rapid Park Chapter of the Future Farmers of America.

I move the adoption of this resolution."

OH 2-1

THE MAIN MOTION

1) RISE AND ADDRESS THE CHAIR

2) GAIN RECOGNITION FROM THE CHAIR

3) MAKE THE MOTION -- "I MOVE THAT . . . "

4) MOTION IS SECONDED

5) CHAIR RESTATES MOTION, ITS ESSENTIAL DESCRIPTIVE CHARACTERISTICS, AND IF DEBATABLE, OPENS DEBATE

6) GAIN RECOGNITION FROM CHAIR FOR DEBATE
   -- MAKER OF THE MOTION HAS PRIORITY
   -- MEMBERS WHO HAVE NOT SPOKEN HAVE PRIORITY OVER THOSE WHO HAVE

7) CHAIR ASKS FOR MORE DISCUSSION BEFORE CLOSING DISCUSSION

8) CHAIR RESTATES THE MOTION

9) VOTE

10) CHAIR STATES EFFECT OF VOTE AND SEALS WITH TAP OF GAVEL (THE TAP OF THE GAVEL IS OPTIONAL)

LESSON 3

COURSE:

UNIT: Leadership

PROBLEM AREA: Parliamentary Procedure - (Subsidiary Motions)

PROBLEM: What are the essential characteristics of subsidiary motions and what procedures are used in making the motion to postpone indefinitely?

OUTCOMES:
1. To describe a subsidiary motion.
2. To list the seven subsidiary motions in order of precedence.
3. To describe the characteristics of each subsidiary motion.
4. To describe in detail the motion to postpone indefinitely.

REFERENCE: Robert's Rules of Order

Key Question #1

What is the definition of a subsidiary motion?

Subsidiary motions are motions applied to other motions for the purpose of most appropriately disposing of them. By them, the original main motion may be modified, action postponed, referred to a committee, etc.

Key Question #2

List the seven subsidiary motions from highest to lowest rank in precedence and the basic characteristic(s) of each.

Motion	Second Required	Debatable	Amend.	Vote Req.	Purpose
Lay on the table	yes	no	no	M	To temporarily set business aside
Previous question	yes	no	no	2/3	To close debate and vote
Limit or extend debate	yes	no	yes	2/3	(extend) To limit time for debate
Postpone to a certain time	yes	yes	yes	M	To delay action
Commit or refer to a committee	yes	yes	yes	M	To place business in the hands of a committee
Amend	yes	yes	once	M	To modify or alter motion
Postpone indefinitely	yes	yes	no	M	To kill motion without vote

Key Question #3

Explain order of precendence again, please.

    Using the chart (Key Question #2) the following could happen:

        Move to buy a flag - second;
        Move to postpone indefinitely - second;
        Move to amend by inserting word "two" - second;
        Move to refer to a committee, second - carried.

    This was possible because each subsequent motion carried a higher order of precedence than the prior one.

    The following would not be correct:

        Move to buy a flag - second;
        Move to postpone to next regular meeting - second;
        Move to refer to a committee

    The motion <u>to refer to a committee</u> is out of order because it does not take precedence over postpone to a certain time.

Key Question #4

What is the purpose of the motion to postpone indefinitely?

This motion is used to reject or kill a main motion without bringing it to a direct vote. It is the lowest ranking of the subsidiary motions. However, if an individual has used up his opportunities to speak, it does give him an additional chance to speak. Form of motion: "**I move to postpone the matter concerning the current topic indefinitely.**"

Key Question #5

What are the qualifications for a motion to postpone indefinitely?

It requires a second, it is debatable, it is not amendable, and it requires a majority vote.

It is not amendable because this would make it another motion. Unlike most other motions, debate can be on the main motion, as well as on the motion to postpone indefinitely.

OH 3-1

SUBSIDIARY MOTION

MOTION	SEC	DEB	AMEND	VOTE	REMARKS
1					
2					
3					
4					
5					
6					

OH 3-2

ARE THE FOLLOWING SITUATIONS IN ORDER?

SITUATION #1

- MOVE TO BUY A FLAG - SECONDED

- MOVE TO POSTPONE INDEFINITELY - SECONDED

- MOVE TO AMMEND BY INSERTING THE WORD "TWO" - SECONDED

- MOVE TO REFER TO A COMMITTEE, SECONDED - CARRIED

- WHY?

SITUATION #2

- MOVE TO BUY A FLAG - SECONDED

- MOVE TO POSTPONE TO NEXT REGULAR MEETING - SECONDED

- MOVE TO REFER TO A COMMITTEE, SECONDED - CARRIED

- WHY?

POSTPONE INDEFINITELY

QUALIFICATIONS: REQUIRES SECOND

IS DEBATABLE

IS NOT AMENDABLE

PURPOSE: TO REJECT OR KILL A MAIN MOTION WITHOUT BRINGING IT TO A DIRECT VOTE.

EXAMPLE: MR./MADAM PRESIDENT, I MOVE TO POSTPONE THE QUESTION INDEFINITELY.

LESSON 4

COURSE:

UNIT: Leadership

PROBLEM AREA: Parliamentary Procedure - (Subsidiary Motions)

PROBLEM: What are the essential features in making the motions of: Amend and Commit?

OUTCOMES:
1. To describe in detail the motion, to amend a main motion.
2. To describe in detail the motion, to refer a question or motion to a committee.

REFERENCE: Robert's Rules of Order

Key Question #1

What is the purpose of the motion to amend?

> When amending, we will change or modify a motion without changing the original main motion's primary intent.

Key Question #2

What four different methods can be used in amending?

> a. Strike out.
> b. Insert or add.
> c. Strike out and insert.
> d. Substitute (entire paragraph or resolution).

Key Question #3

How many amendments can be on the floor at one time?

> Two amendmends can be on the floor at one time -- the first being the primary amendment and the second the secondary amendment. The first must be germane (pertaining to) to the main motion and the second must be germane (pertaining to) to the primary amendment.
>
> Special rules pertaining to relevance and the number of special amendments are adopted by some deliberative assemblies.

Key Question #4

What are the qualifications for the motion to amend?

>It requires a second, it is debatable, it is amendable, but only to the second degree; and it requires a majority vote.

Key Question #5

What is the proper form to use when amending?

>**"I move to amend the motion or amendment by (adding), (striking out) or (striking and inserting) the word . . ."**

Key Question #6

Write an abbreviated dialogue of an amendment to an amendment.

Member: "I move our organization buy a flag" - seconded.

Chair: "It has been moved and seconded that our organization purchase a flag. This motion is debatable, amendable and requires a majority vote. Is there any discussion?"

Member: "I move to amend the main motion by inserting before the word flag, (two plastic)." - seconded.

Chair: "It has been moved and seconded to amend the main motion by . . .* any discussion."

Member: "I move to amend the amendment by striking the word plastic." - seconded

Chair: "It has been moved and seconded to amend the amendment by . . .* any discussion." (Pause) "If none let us vote."
"All in favor say aye." "All opposed say no." "The ayes have it . . . we will amend the amendment by striking the word plastic."

"Is there any discussion on the amendment as amended?" "If not let us vote." "All those in favor of amending the main motion with the amended amendment by inserting the word two, say aye." "Those opposed say no." "The ayes have it. The main motion will be amended by adding the word two before flag."

"Is there any discussion on the main motion as amended which states . . . ?*" "If not let us vote -- those in favor say aye, those opposed say no." The ayes have it and the motion as amended passes. Our organization will buy two flags."

* Note -- The chair should state at each of these instances the motion and the essential descriptive characteristics of the motions -- (debatable, amendable, vote required).

18

Key Question #7

What is the purpose of the motion to refer to a committee?

> The purpose of this motion is to place business in the hands of a few members so that more information can be obtained on it or so that it can be acted on more effectively. Committees should have people from both sides of the issue.

Key Question #8

What specifications must be included in a motion to commit?

   a. Which committee (special or standing)?
   b. What powers?
   c. If special -- how many members?
   d. If special -- how appointed?

Key Question #9

What power options are available to the committee?

   a. Full power to act.
   b. Investigate and report back.
   c. Investigate, report and recommend.

Key Question #10

What are the qualifications on the motion to refer to a committee?

> It requires a second, is amendable, and debatable, it requires a majority vote.

Key Question #11

How may a committee be selected?

   a. Appointed by chair.
   b. Appointed by maker of motion.
   c. Volunteers.
   d. Nominations and ballot.
   e. Nominations and voice vote.

Key Question #12

When does a committee report to the membership?

> Unless otherwise specified, the committee presents a report at the meeting immediately following its formation and at every regular meeting thereafter until discharged, dissolved or its work is completed.

OH 4-1

AMEND

QUALIFICATIONS: SECOND REQUIRED
                                      AMENDABLE ONCE
                                      DEBATABLE
                                      MAJORITY VOTE

PURPOSE: CHANGE OR MODIFY A MOTION

MEANS AVAILABLE:
1. STRIKE OUT
2. INSERT OR ADD
3. STRIKE OUT AND INSERT
4. SUBSTITUTE - MUST BE AN ENTIRE MOTION OR A FULL PARAGRAPH

TWO AMENDMENTS MAY BE ON THE FLOOR AT ONE TIME, THE FIRST BEING THE PRIMARY AMENDMENT, THE SECOND BEING THE SECONDARY AMENDMENT. THE FIRST MUST BE GERMANE TO THE MAIN MOTION, THE SECOND GERMANE TO THE PRIMARY AMENDMENT.

EXAMPLE: I MOVE TO AMEND THE MAIN MOTION BY ADDING 500 PEOPLE AT 4 O'CLOCK. I MOVE TO AMEND THE AMENDMENT BY STRIKING THE WORDS, AT 4 O'CLOCK, AND INSERTING AT 3 O'CLOCK.

OH 4-1

COMMIT OR REFER

QUALIFICATIONS: REQUIRES SECOND
AMENDABLE
DEBATABLE
MAJORITY VOTE

PURPOSE: GAIN MORE INFORMATION
ACT ON MEASURE MORE EFFECTIVELY

EXAMPLE: I MOVE TO REFER THIS MATTER (MOTION OR QUESTION) TO THE MEMBERSHIP COMMITTEE.

- IF MOTION IS SIMPLY: I MOVE TO REFER THE QUESTION TO A COMMITTEE.

- PRESIDENT ASKS:

    A) WHAT COMMITTEE?   STANDING
       SPECIAL

    B) IF SPECIAL, HOW IS IT TO BE APPOINTED?

    C) NUMBER DESIRED ON COMMITTEE

    D) THEIR POWER

-- UNLESS SPECIFIED, COMMITTEE REPORT IS PRESENTED AT NEXT MEETING.

LESSON 5

COURSE:

UNIT: Leadership

PROBLEM AREA: Parliamentary Procedure - (<u>Subsidiary Motions</u>)

PROBLEM: What are the essential features in making the motions of: <u>postponing to a certain time</u>, <u>limit or extend time for debate</u>, <u>previous question</u>, and <u>lay on the table</u>.

OUTCOMES:
1. To describe in detail the motion <u>to postpone to a certain time</u>.
2. To describe in detail the motion <u>to limit or extend time for debate</u>.
3. To describe in detail the motion <u>to call for the previous question</u>.
4. To describe in detail the motion <u>to lay the pending question on the table</u>.

REFERENCE: <u>Robert's Rules of Order</u>

Key Question #1

What are the three purposes of the motion to <u>postpone definitely (postpone to a certain time)</u>?

> The motion to postpone definitely has a three-fold purpose. The first being to delay action on a given item of business, the second, is to set up a definite time to consider the motion which is set aside, and third, is that we have some means of setting an item aside for something which is more important.

Key Question #2

Where should something that is <u>postponed definitely</u> show up?

> If it is postponed until the next meeting, it should show up on the agenda as unfinished business.

Key Question #3

What are the qualifications on the motion to <u>postpone definitely</u>?

> It does require a second, it is debatable, it is amendable as to the time to which it will be postponed and it normally requires a majority vote.

Key Question #4

What form is used to present the motion to postpone to a certain time?

> Member: "I move that we postpone the pending question until our next regular meeting."

Key Question #5

What is the purpose of the motion to limit or extend time for debate?

> This motion has two purposes which are directly opposite of each other.
>
> a. It can be made to hold down unnecessary debate and a lengthy discussion.
> b. It can be made to provide for additional discussion time.

Key Question #6

What methods do we have by which to limit or extend debate?

> Either by reducing or lengthening the normal length or number of speeches or by having debate closed at a certain hour or after a specified period of time.

Key Question #7

What are the qualifications of the motion to limit or extend time for debate?

> A second is required, it is amendable as to the time or length of speaking, it is not debatable since this would defeat the purpose of the motion, and it requires a two-thirds vote, since if it passes it could take away someone's speaking rights.

Key Question #8

What form is used to present the motion to limit time for debate?

> Member: "I move that our organization limit time for debate on the pending question to two speeches in favor of and two speeches against the motion."

Key Question #9

What form is used to present the motion to extend time for debate?

> This motion is most commonly used to extend debate after debate has been stopped due to a previous motion to limit time for debate for a specific length of time or number of speeches.
>
> Member: "I move to extend time for debate for ten more minutes."

Key Question #10

What is the purpose of the motion to call for the previous question?

This motion has the function of stopping all debate and bringing items of business to an immediate vote. It prevents any other subsidiary motions except lay on the table from being made.

Key Question #11

What will the motion of previous question apply to?

This motion can be applied to any motion which is amendable or debatable but the mover must specify if she wants to have it apply to more than the immediate pending motion, i.e. just the pending amendment or to all motions pending on the current topic.

Key Question #12

What is the correct form for stating the motion previous question?

"I move the previous question," is the only correct form by which to make the motion. The term Question is only a term which indicates a readiness to vote, although it may be used for this purpose, the chair should not recognize it as the formal motion. If she does, she is technically incorrect. It serves no real purpose and is really only a disruption in the meeting or an indication that the speaker of the term Question is ready to vote.

Key Question #13

What are the qualifications of the motion to call for the previous question?

In order for the motion to be brought before the assembly one other person must feel the same way; therefore, a second is required, but no amendments or debate can be applied to the motion. Because of this, and the fact that if the motion passes you will be infringing on someone else's rights, it requires a two-thirds vote.

Key Question #14

What is the purpose of the motion to lay on the table?

The purpose of this motion is to lay an item of business aside temporarily, so an item of business which is more urgent can be handled.

Key Question #15

How does the motion to lay on the table differ from the motion to postpone definitely?

> First of all, it has different qualifications than the motion to postpone definitely. Second, when one postpones definitely the item automatically comes up on the agenda at the time it was postponed to. If the motion layed on the table is not brought up at the next regular meeting or during the same meeting, it will be lost. At times, the motion to lay on the table is misused when the person's intent was to kill a motion. In order to bring an item of business back after it has been layed on the table requires the unclassified motion of to take from the table. This too, requires a majority vote.

Key Question #16

What are the qualifications of the motion to lay on the table?

> It requires a second, is not amendable or debatable and requires a majority vote. A majority vote is all that is necessary because the item can be brought back with the same majority vote.

Key Question #17

What form is used to present the motion to lay on the table?

> Member: **"I move to lay the pending motion on the table."**

Key Question #18

What are the subsidiary motions in the order of highest to lowest precedence.

- L - Lay on the table
- P - Previous question
- L - Limit or extend time for debate
- P - Postpone definitely
- C - Commit or refer
- A - Amend
- P - Postpone indefinitely

OH 5-1

POSTPONE DEFINITELY

(POSTPONE TO A CERTAIN TIME)

QUALIFICATIONS: REQUIRES SECOND
  DEBATABLE
  AMENDABLE
  MAJORITY VOTE

PURPOSES: DELAY ACTION TO A CERTAIN TIME

  TO SET A TIME WHEN A MATTER MUST BE DISCUSSED

  TO MAKE TIME FOR MORE PRESSING BUSINESS

EXAMPLE: "I MOVE THAT THE QUESTION BE POSTPONED TO THE NEXT MEETING."

OR "I MOVE THAT THE QUESTION BE POSTPONED TO 3:00 P.M."

OH 5-2

LIMIT OR EXTEND DEBATE

QUALIFICATIONS: REQUIRES SECOND
AMENDABLE
NOT DEBATABLE
2/3 VOTE

PURPOSE: HOLD DOWN LENGTHY DISCUSSION, OR PROVIDE ADDITIONAL TIME FOR DISCUSSION.

EXAMPLE: "I MOVE THAT DEBATE ON THE PENDING QUESTION BE LIMITED TO 20 MINUTES."

OR   "I MOVE THAT DEBATE ON THE PENDING QUESTION BE LIMITED TO ONE SPEECH."

OR   "I MOVE THAT . . . BE LIMITED TO FIVE MINUTES FROM EACH SIDE."

OR   "I MOVE THAT MR. X'S SPEECH BE LIMITED TO FIVE MINUTES."

EXAMPLE: "I MOVE THAT MR. X BE ALLOWED TO EXTEND HIS DEBATE TIME FIVE MORE MINUTES."

OH 5-3

PREVIOUS QUESTION

QUALIFICATIONS: REQUIRES SECOND
NOT DEBATABLE
NOT AMENDABLE
2/3 VOTE

PURPOSE: STOP DEBATE AND VOTE

EXAMPLE: "I MOVE THE PREVIOUS QUESTION."

    NOT: "QUESTION" - THIS ONLY INDICATES ONE MEMBER IS READY FOR VOTE.

-- MAY BE CONFINED TO AN AMENDMENT, WITHOUT AFFECTING THE MAIN MOTION.

OH 5-4

LAY ON THE TABLE

QUALIFICATIONS: REQUIRES SECOND
NOT DEBATABLE
NOT AMENDABLE
MAJORITY VOTE

PURPOSE: TO LAY ASIDE AN ITEM OF BUSINESS TEMPORARILY IN ORDER TO ATTEND TO MORE URGENT BUSINESS.

EXAMPLE: "I MOVE TO LAY THE QUESTION ON THE TABLE."

-- MUST BE BROUGHT UP AT NEXT MEETING OR IT DIES.

-- REQUIRES UNCLASSIFIED MOTION OF TAKE FROM THE TABLE (TO RESTORE).

-- CANNOT BE QUALIFIED. (OR IT IS POSTPONED INDEFINITELY)

LESSON 6

COURSE:

UNIT: Leadership

PROBLEM AREA: Parliamentary Procedure - (Privileged Motions)

PROBLEM: What are the essential characteristics of privileged motions in general and specifically each of the five individual motions?

OUTCOMES:
1. To describe privileged motions.
2. To list the five privileged motions in order of precedence.
3. To describe in detail the motion to call for the orders of the day.
4. To describe in detail the motion to raise a question of privilege.
5. To describe in detail the motion to take a recess.
6. To describe in detail the motion to adjourn.
7. To describe in detail the motion to fix time to which to adjourn.

REFERENCE: Robert's Rules of Order

Key Question #1

What is the definition of a privileged motion?

> Privileged motions are unlike subsidiary and incidental motions in that they do not relate to the pending questions. As privileged questions, they are, however, of much importance and take precedence over all other motions. Privileged motions are undebatable but do have an **order of precedence**.

Key Qusetion #2

List the <u>five privileged motions</u> in order of precedence and the basic essential descriptive characteristics of each.

Privileged Motions

Motion	Second Required	Debatable	Amend.	Vote Req.	Purpose
Fix time to which to adjourn	yes	no	yes	M	To set time for next meeting
Adjourn	yes	no	no	M	To end meeting
Take a recess	yes	no	yes	M	Provide an intermission to interrupt a meeting
Raise a question of privilege	no	no	no	None	To obtain action immediately in an emergency
Orders of the day	no	no	no	None or neg. 2/3	To force the chair to conduct business in correct order

Key Question #3

What is the purpose of the motion <u>to call for the orders of the day</u>?

It is really a demand for the group to follow the agenda which has been set up, and therefore, it is only in order when the agenda is not being followed in its proper proposed order.

Key Question #4

What qualifications must the motion <u>to call for the orders of the day follow</u>?

This motion requires no second, is not amendable or debatable and requires no vote under most circumstances; however, if the assembly does not wish to return to the orders of the day, in order to continue with its current business it must defeat the motion by a <u>negative two-thirds vote</u>.

Key Question #5

How should the motion to call for the orders of the day be stated?

    Member: "**I call for the orders of the day.**"
    Chair: "**The orders of the day have been called for; therefore, we will return to following the orders of the day.**"

Key Question #6

What happens if the organization and/or chair wish to vote on whether or not they wish to return to the agenda?

    Chair: "**Those in favor of returning to the orders of the day (agenda) raise your . . . those opposed raise . . . hand. Since a 2/3 negative vote has not been met, we will return to the proposed agenda.**"

    or   "**There being a two-thirds vote in the negative, we will not return to the orders of the day, but will continue with our current business.**"

Key Question #7

What is the purpose of the motion question of privilege?

    This motion permits a request to be brought up before the assembly immediately. This can either be a privilege for the assembly or a personal privilege.

Key Question #8

What qualifications must a question of privilege meet?

    It does not require a second, is not debatable or amendable and is ruled upon or disposed of by the chair.

Key Question #9

How should a question of privilege be stated?

    Member: "**Mr./Madam President, I rise to a question of personal privilege,**" or "**. . . privilege for the assembly.**"

    Chair: "**State your question.**"

    Member states her question (generally relates to comfort, noise, sound systems, etc.) and the chair rules on it.

Key Question #10

What is the purpose of the motion to take a recess?

This motion is usually made so that a short intermission can take place, wherein many different types of operations can be performed.

Key Question #11

What qualifications cover the motion to take a recess?

It requires a second, it is not debatable, is amendable as to the length of time, and requires a majority vote.

If no other business is pending when the motion to take a recess is made, it then becomes a regular main motion with all the qualifications of a main motion (debatable, amendable, majority vote).

Key Question #12

What form is used in presenting the motion to recess?

Member: "I move we recess for five minutes."

Key Question #13

What is the purpose of the motion to adjourn?

This motion has the effect of closing the meeting.

Key Question #14

What are the qualifications on the motion to adjourn?

As a privileged motion it is not amendable, not debatable and requires a majority vote. It requires a second as well.

When the motion to adjourn becomes a main motion, it then has the same qualifications as a regular main motion (debatable, amendable, majority vote).

The motion, to adjourn, can become a main motion under the following conditions: When the motion is qualified in any way as to set a time to adjourn, or when a time to adjourn has already been established, or when the effect of the motion would be to dissolve the assembly.

Key Question #15

What is the purpose of the motion to fix the time to which to adjourn?

> The purpose is to set the time for another meeting; it has no effect on when the current meeting will adjourn.

Key Question #16

When should the motion to fix the time to which to adjourn be made?

> It should be made when another meeting is needed but which is not already scheduled. If it is made when another meeting is already scheduled, it should be ruled out of order. If it is made when no other motion is on the floor, it then becomes a main motion, thus having all qualifications of a main motion.

Key Question #17

What are the qualifications of the motion to fix time to which to adjourn?

> The motion requires a second, is not debatable, is amendable and requires a majority vote.
>
> - amendments are not debatable
> - amendable only as to time and place

Mover:	"**I move that when we adjourn, we stand adjourned to meet at (until) 8:00 a.m. on Tuesday, June 2 at the High School.**"
If it passes:	"**When we adjourn we will reconvene at 8:00 a.m. . . . .**"

OH 6-1

PRIVILEGED MOTIONS

F - TO FIX THE TIME TO WHICH TO ADJOURN

A - TO ADJOURN

T - TO TAKE A RECESS

R - TO RISE TO A QUESTION OF PRIVILEGE

O - TO CALL FOR THE ORDERS OF THE DAY

OH 6-2

ORDERS OF THE DAY

PURPOSE: IS A DEMAND FOR THE GROUP TO FOLLOW THE AGENDA.

QUALIFICATIONS: IF ASSEMBLY DOESN'T WISH TO RETURN TO ORDERS OF DAY, MUST DEFEAT MOTION BY NEGATIVE 2/3 VOTE.

QUESTION OF PRIVILEGE

PURPOSE: PERMITS PERSONAL OR GROUP PRIVILEGE REQUEST TO BE BROUGHT UP BEFORE ASSEMBLY IMMEDIATELY.

- IS RULED ON BY THE CHAIR

TO TAKE A RECESS

PURPOSE: TO TAKE A SHORT BREAK

QUALIFICATIONS: REQUIRES SECOND
NOT DEBATABLE
AMENDABLE

- IS A MAIN MOTION WHEN NO OTHER BUSINESS IS PENDING.

OH 6-3

ADJOURN

PURPOSE: TO CLOSE MEETING

QUALIFICATIONS: REQUIRES SECOND
　　　　　　　　　NOT AMENDABLE
　　　　　　　　　NOT DEBATABLE
　　　　　　　　　MAJORITY VOTE

- BECOMES MAIN MOTION WHEN QUALIFIED

TO FIX THE TIME TO WHICH TO ADJOURN

PURPOSE: TO SET TIME FOR ANOTHER MEETING. HAS NO EFFECT ON WHEN THE CURRENT MEETING ADJOURNS (ENDS).

QUALIFICATIONS: REQUIRES SECOND
　　　　　　　　　NOT DEBATABLE
　　　　　　　　　AMENDABLE
　　　　　　　　　MAJORITY VOTE

E.G.   I MOVE THAT WHEN WE ADJOURN WE ADJOURN UNTIL 8:00 A.M. TUESDAY AT THE HIGH SCHOOL

LESSON 7

COURSE:

UNIT: Leadership

PROBLEM AREA: Parliamentary Procedure - (Incidental Motions)

PROBLEM: What are the essential descriptive characteristics of incidental motions in general and specifically the five request motions: parliamentary inquiry, point of information, withdraw or modify a motion, to read papers, and to be excused from duty?

OUTCOMES:
1. To describe incidental motions.
2. To list the incidental motions and their basic essential descriptive characteristics.
3. To describe in detail the motion to make a parliamentary inquiry.
4. To describe in detail the motion to rise to a point of information.
5. To describe in detail the motion to withdraw or modify a motion.
6. To describe in detail the motion to read a paper.
7. To describe in detail the motion to be excused from duty.

REFERENCE: Robert's Rules of Order

Key Question #1

What is the definition of incidental motions?

Incidental motions may be defined as:

a. Arising from another motion or transaction on which they have a bearing.
b. Having no definite order of precedence among themselves.
c. Having precedence over Subsidiary and Main motions.
d. Helping to transact business and to insure fair play.
e. Undebatable, except an appeal under certain circumstances.
f. Generally, not amendable.
g. Are in order when they logically pertain to any motion before the assembly.
h. Are individually decided as each is presented.

Key Question #2

List the incidental motions and the essential descriptive characteristics of each.

Incidental Motions

Motion	Second Required	Debatable	Amend.	Vote Req.	Purpose
Parliamentary inquiry	no	no	no	None	Seek parliamentary information
Request for information	no	no	no	None	Information on motion
Withdraw a motion	no	no	no	no/yes	Withdraw a motion before a vote
Read a paper or manuscript	yes	no	no	M	Delay action
Request to be excused	no	no	no	Unanimous	To be excused from duty
Point of order	no	no	no	None	Insure orderly procedure
Quorum	no	no	no	None	Determine legality to take action
Division of assembly	no	no	no	None	Verify vote
Divide a question	yes	no	yes	M	Separation of items
Object to consideration of question	no	no	no	2/3	Suppress action
Suspend the rules	yes	no	no	2/3	Violate rules
Close nominations	yes	no	yes	2/3	Close nominations
Reopen nominations	yes	no	yes	M	Add names
Choose a method of voting	yes	no	yes	M	Decide method
Appeal from decision of chair	yes	yes/no	no	M	Determine correctness of chair's decision

Key Question #3

What is the purpose of the motion to make a parliamentary inquiry?

The purpose of this motion is to request, of the presiding officer, information relating to parliamentary law or rules of the organization affecting the business at hand.

Key Question #4

What are the essential descriptive characteristics of the motion to make a parliamentary inquiry?

A member need not be recognized when making the motion and no second is required. This motion is not debatable, not amendable and no vote is required.

Key Question #5

What form is used in stating the motion to make a parliamentary inquiry?

Member:	"I rise to a parliamentary inquiry."
Chair:	"The member will state her inquiry."
Member:	"Is it proper . . . ?" "Does the motion to . . . . affect . . . ?"

Key Question #6

What is the purpose of the motion to request information?

The purpose of this motion is to serve as a method of properly securing the floor to ask a question pertaining to the motion being discussed.

Key Question #7

What are the essential descriptive characteristics of the motion?

If a point is raised when another has the floor, he must ask and receive permission from the speaker in order to interrupt. The motion does not require a second, is not debatable or amendable, and is not voted on.

Key Question #8

What form is used in stating the motion to request information?

Member:	"I rise to a point of information."
Chair:	"The member will state her point."
Member:	"Does the treasury . . . ?" "Would the speaker please tell us about . . . relating to the motion."

Key Question #9

What is the purpose of the motion <u>to request permission to withdraw or modify a motion</u>?

> Before the chair states the motion the mover can do anything he wishes.
>
> If the motion is given to the group, there must be unanimous consent of the group to change or modify it unless the motion to amend is used. After a question is divided, parts of it may be withdrawn.
>
> If there is no objection or if the request is made before the motion is restated by the chair; no second is needed, the motion is not debatable nor amendable, and requires no vote.
>
> The motion <u>to request permission to withdraw or modify a motion</u> is generally a courtesy motion used to speed up business transactions and eliminate unnecessary parliamentary entanglements.

Key Question #10

What form is used in stating the motion <u>to request to withdraw a motion</u>?

> Member: **"I request permission to withdraw the pending motion."**
> Chair: **"Unless there is an objection (pause) the motion is withdrawn."**

Key Question #11

What is the purpose of the motion <u>to request to read a paper</u>?

> The purpose of this motion is to permit a member to read (or prevent one from reading) a lengthy paper as a form of discussion on a motion.

Key Question #12

What are the essential descriptive characteristics of the motion <u>to read a paper</u>?

> If any member objects, a member has no right to read from -- or to have the secretary read from -- any paper or book as a part of his speech without the permission of the assembly.
>
> The motion to read a paper requires a second and majority vote. The motion is not debatable or amendable.

Key Question #13

What form is used in stating the motion to read a paper?

> Member: "Madam President, I request permission to read a statement in debate of . . . "
> Chair: "Unless there is an objection (pause) the member may read . . . "
> OR
> Chair: **"Because of the objection we will vote, a majority vote is necessary to allow the paper to be read."**

Key Question #14

What is the purpose of the motion to request to be excused from duty?

> The informal form of this motion is to request to be excused from serving on a committee, etc., at the time of appointment.

Key Question #15

What are the essential descriptive characteristics of the motion to request to be excused from duty?

> Unless the bylaws of an organization impose specific duties on a member beyond the mere payment of dues, she may decline any duty at the time of appointment.
>
> If the bylaws state that a duty must be accepted, the member can only be relieved of duty by unanimous consent or resignation.
>
> In general, the informal motion does not need a second, a vote, and is not debatable or amendable.

Key Question #16

What form is used for the motion to request to be excused from duty?

> Chair: "I appoint Sue, John . . . "
> Member: "I request to be excused from duty as I . . . "
> Chair: **"Sue is excused, I appoint Mary in her place."**

OH 7-1

INCIDENTAL MOTIONS

PARLIAMENTARY INQUIRY

POINT OF INFORMATION

PERMISSION TO WITHDRAW OR MODIFY A MOTION

REQUEST PAPERS TO BE READ

EXCUSE FROM DUTY

POINT OF ORDER

QUORUM

DIVISION OF THE ASSEMBLY

DIVIDE THE QUESTION

OBJECTION TO THE CONSIDERATION OF THE QUESTION

SUSPEND THE RULES

TO CLOSE NOMINATIONS

TO REOPEN NOMINATIONS

TO CHOOSE A METHOD OF VOTING

APPEAL THE DECISION OF THE CHAIR

OH 7-2

PARLIAMENTARY INQUIRY

QUALIFICATIONS: NO SECOND
                  NOT DEBATABLE
                  NOT AMENDABLE
                  NO VOTE

PURPOSE: SEEK PARLIAMENTARY INFORMATION

EXAMPLE: "I RISE TO A PARLIAMENTARY INQUIRY."

REQUEST INFORMATION

QUALIFICATIONS: NO SECOND
                  NOT DEBATABLE
                  NOT AMENDABLE
                  NO VOTE

PURPOSE: TO ASK A QUESTION ABOUT THE MOTION ON THE FLOOR.

EXAMPLE: "I RISE TO A POINT OF INFORMATION."

WITHDRAW (OR MODIFY) A MOTION

QUALIFICATIONS:
- NO SECOND
- NOT DEBATABLE
- NOT AMENDABLE
- NO VOTE (UNLESS AN OBJECTION IS RAISED)

PURPOSE: TO REMOVE (OR MODIFY) A MOTION ON THE FLOOR BEFORE IT IS BROUGHT UP FOR A VOTE.

EXAMPLE: "I REQUEST PERMISSION TO WITHDRAW (OR MODIFY) THE PENDING QUESTION."

READ A PAPER

QUALIFICATIONS:
- REQUIRES A SECOND
- NOT DEBATABLE
- NOT AMENDABLE
- REQUIRES A MAJORITY VOTE

PURPOSE: TO OBTAIN PERMISSION TO READ A LENGTHY STATEMENT OR PAPER AS DEBATE ON A PENDING MOTION.

EXAMPLE: "MR. PRESIDENT, I REQUEST PERMISSION TO READ A PAPER IN DEBATE OF . . ."

OH 7-4

REQUEST TO BE EXCUSED FROM DUTY

QUALIFICATIONS: NOT SECONDED
NOT DEBATABLE
NOT AMENDABLE
UNANIMOUS OR NO VOTE

PURPOSE: TO MAKE A FORMAL REQUEST TO BE EXCUSED FROM SERVING.

EXAMPLE: MEMBER: "I REQUEST TO BE EXCUSED FROM THIS DUTY."

LESSON 8

COURSE:

UNIT: Leadership

PROBLEM AREA: Parliamentary Procedure - (Incidental Motion)

PROBLEM: What are the essential descriptive characteristics of incidental motions <u>to rise to a point of order</u>, <u>determine a quorum</u>, <u>division of the assembly</u>, <u>divide a question</u>, <u>object to the consideration</u>, <u>suspend the rules</u>, <u>close nominations</u>, <u>reopen nominations</u>, <u>choose a method of voting</u>, and <u>appeal from the decision of the chair</u>.

OUTCOMES:
1. To describe in detail the motion <u>to rise to a point of order</u>.
2. To describe in detail the motion <u>to determine a quorum</u>.
3. To describe in detail the motion <u>to call for a division of the assembly</u>.
4. To describe in detail the motion <u>to divide a question and consider by parts</u>.
5. To describe in detail the motion <u>to object to the consideration of a question</u>.
6. To describe in detail the motion <u>to suspend the rules</u>.
7. To describe in detail the motion <u>to close nominations</u>.
8. To describe in detail the motion <u>to reopen nominations</u>.
9. To describe in detail the motion <u>to choose a method of voting</u>.
10. To describe in detail the motion <u>to appeal from the decision of the chair</u>.

REFERENCE: <u>Robert's Rules of Order</u>

Key Question #1

What is the purpose of the motion <u>to rise to a point of order</u>?

To enforce the rules of parliamentary law and the rules of the organization by bringing some **breach of the law** to the attention of the presiding officer. The presiding officer rules the motion, or breach, **out of** or **in** order as he determines. The presiding officer <u>does not rule the person out of order</u>.

Key Question #2

What are the essential descriptive characteristics of the motion <u>to rise to a point of order</u>?

This motion does not require a second, it is not amendable or debatable and is generally ruled on by the president, but if the chair does not wish to make a ruling, it can be decided on by a majority vote.

Key Question #3

What form is used in stating the motion to rise to a point of order?

    Member: **"Point of order Mr./Madam President,"** or **"Point of order,"** or **"I rise to a point of order."**
    Chair: **"State your point."**
    Member: States the matter that she believes is wrong. **"The motion to . . . does not take precedence over . . . "**
    Chair: **"Your point is well taken and . . . "** or **"Your point is not well taken in that . . . "**

Key Question #4

What is the purpose of the motion point of order in doubting a quorum?

    A quorum in an assembly is the number of members entitled to vote who must be present in order that business can be legally transacted. It is the chair's responsibility to determine the presence of a quorum before opening the meeting and to oversee the presence of a quorum during the meeting. However, if a member doubts the presence of a quorum she may use this motion.

Key Question #5

What are the essential descriptive characteristics of the motion to doubt a quorum?

    This motion does not require a second, is not debatable or amendable, and no vote is required.

Key Question #6

What form is used in stating the motion to doubt a quorum?

    Member: **"Mr./Madam Chair, I rise to a point of order -- I doubt the presence of a quorum."**

Key Question #7

What is the purpose of the motion to call for a division of the assembly?

    The purpose of this motion is to obtain a more accurate vote, when a voice vote was previously taken, and it appeared close.

    In order to constitute a true division of the assembly the revote must be taken by a counted vote.

Key Question #8

What are the essential descriptive characteristics of the motion to call for a division of the assembly?

>It is not amendable, not debatable, and no second or vote is taken on whether or not to take the revote.

Key Question #9

What form is used in stating the motion to call for a division of the assembly?

>Immediately after a vote has been taken and up until another motion is made. It can be called for by stating: **"I call for a division."** whereupon, the chair revotes with a counted vote.

Key Question #10

What is the purpose of the motion to divide a question and consider by parts?

>To separate a complex or double motion into two, which when separated can stand alone without the need of the other part.

>For example, "I move we have a speaker and a movie at our next meeting." This is a divisible question.

Key Question #11

What are the essential descriptive characteristics of the motion to divide a question and consider by parts?

>It yields to all subsidiary motions except postpone indefinitely, amend, limit or extend time of debate, privileged, and applicable incidental motions.

>A second is required, it is amendable, not debatable, and requires a majority vote.

Key Question #12

What form is used in stating the motion to divide a question and consider by parts?

>(See Key Question #10)
>Member: **"I move that we divide the question and consider it as two motions; the first, that we have a speaker at our next meeting; and second, that we have a movie at our next meeting."**

49

Key Question #13

What is the purpose of the motion to object to the consideration of the question?

The purpose of this motion is to prevent an item of business from being formally considered by the assembly.

Key Question #14

What are the essential descriptive characteristics of the motion to object to the consideration of a question?

This motion must be made before any discussion has occurred on the original main motion. It yields to the motion to lay on the table. If the motion to lay on the table is made, while the objection is on the floor, both the objection and the main motion are layed on the table if the later passes. The presiding officer can make the objection. Illegal, inappropriate and/or seemingly offensive motions are nearly always objected to.

The objection requires no second, there can be no amendments or debate, and it requires a two-thirds negative vote.

Key Question #15

What form is used in stating the motion to object to the consideration of the question?

Member "A":	"I move we require H.I.V. testing for new members." "Seconded."
Member "B":	"I object to the consideration of this question."
Chairperson:	"The consideration of the question has been objected to. An objection requires a 2/3 negative vote to not consider the question. Shall the question be considered? Those in favor of considering it, please rise . . . be seated. Those opposed . . . to considering the question, rise, be seated."

Chairperson calls the vote.

"A 2/3's negative vote has been met, so we will not consider . . . "

Key Question #16

What is the purpose of the motion to suspend the rules?

When a group or assembly wishes to do something that it cannot do without violating one or more of its regular rules, it may vote to overlook them for a time. However, the suspension that takes place cannot be in conflict with the organization's constitution, bylaws, or fundamental parliamentary law, unless special parliamentary rules and proper notifications are made.

Key Question #17

What are the essential descriptive characteristics of the motion to suspend the rules?

The motion to suspend the rules yields to all privileged motions and to lay on the table. The only exception in the subsidiary motions is to call for orders of the day.

When a rule or rules are to be suspended, the rule itself is not mentioned, but a specific purpose must be stated as to why something is being suspended.

If the motion to suspend the rules is lost it cannot be renewed for the same purpose at the same meeting. However, after an adjournment it can be brought up again on the same day.

The motion to suspend the rules requires a second, it is not debatable or amendable and requires a two-thirds vote because you are going against the regular functioning of your group.

Key Question #18

What form is used in stating the motion to suspend the rules?

Member: "I move that the local rule be suspended (or "to suspend the rule") which interferes with our sending first year board members to the national convention."

Key Question #19

What is the purpose of the motion to close nominations?

The motion to close nominations in small organizations is often used unnecessarily and even illegally. The motion to close nominations should not be used until considerable time has been given for nominations to be made. It is out of order if a member is still seeking the floor to make a nomination. Nominations automatically close when no more are made. It is illegal to use the motion to close nominations as a way of **"railroading"** a person into a position.

Key Question #20

What are the essential descriptive characteristics of the motion to close nominations?

In order to close nominations you must have a second and a 2/3 vote. It is amendable, but not debatable.

Key Question #21

What form is used in stating the motion to close nominations?

> Member: "**Mr. President, I move that nominations cease, (or be stopped after three more candidates are nominated).**"

Key Question #22

What is the purpose of the motion to reopen nominations?

> At any time for most any reason, before voting takes place the motion to reopen nominations may be made. It is made when someone wants to add names to the ballot.

Key Question #23

What are the essential descriptive characteristics of the motion to reopen nominations?

> This motion requires a second, is not debatable, is amendable and requires a majority vote.

Key Question #24

What form is used to state the motion to reopen nominations?

> Member: "**I move that nominations be reopened.**"

Key Question #25

What is the purpose of the motion to choose a method of voting?

> The object of this motion is to obtain a form of voting other than voice or rising (Division).

Key Question #26

What are the essential descriptive characteristics of the motion to choose a method of voting?

> The motion requires a second, is not debatable, is amendable, and requires a majority vote.

Key Question #27

What form is used in stating the motion to choose a method of voting?

> Member: "**I move that the vote be taken by written ballot.**"

Key Question #28

What is the purpose of the motion <u>to appeal from the decision of the chair</u>?

> In the case where the chair makes a decision with which a member disagrees, this is the motion by which he can disagree with the decision.

Key Question #29

What are the essential descriptive characteristics of the motion <u>to appeal from the decision of the chair</u>?

> An appeal requires a second, is debatable unless the original motion is non-debatable or applies to a transgression of the rules. A majority or tie vote is required to sustain the chair. The motion is not amendable.
>
> The appeal must take place immediately after the ruling or before any other business is brought to the floor. Once the appeal has been made, the chair can justify or give reasons why she made the decision, while presiding.
>
> The motion to appeal from the decision of the chair yields to all privileged motions, yields to any incidental motions which arise out of the appeal itself. It also yields to the subsidiary motions of limit or extend of time for debate, commit, postpone definitely, and previous question only when the original motion which it applies to is debatable and it always yields to lay on the table.

Key Question #30

What form is used in stating the motion <u>to appeal from the decision of the chair</u>?

> Situation: A point of group privilege has been raised regarding the high temperature of the room. The chair denies the request to open a window and continues with the business at hand.
>
> Member: **"Mr. Chairman, I appeal from the decision of the chair."**
>
> Chair: **"An appeal on the decision of not opening the window has been called for. All those in favor of upholding the decision of the chair say "aye . . . those opposed say "no" . . . (The "ayes"/"nos") have it and the decision is (upheld/reversed)."**

OH 8-1

POINT OF ORDER

PURPOSE: TO ENFORCE THE RULES OF PARLIAMENTARY LAW WHEN SOMEONE HAS TAKEN ACTION WITHOUT FOLLOWING CORRECT PARLIAMENTARY PROCEDURES

QUALIFICATIONS: NO SECOND
NOT DEBATABLE
NOT AMENDABLE
NO VOTE

FORM:
- MEMBER: "I RISE TO A POINT OF ORDER."
- CHAIR: "STATE YOUR POINT."
- MEMBER: STATES WHAT HE BELIEVES IS WRONG.
- CHAIR: "YOUR POINT IS WELL TAKEN."
- OR "YOUR POINT IS NOT WELL TAKEN."

OH 8-2

QUORUM

PURPOSE: TO DETERMINE NUMBER OF PEOPLE PRESENT SO BUSINESS CAN BE TRANSACTED LEGALLY.

- CHAIR'S RESPONSIBILITY TO DETERMINE

FORM: "MR./MADAM PRESIDENT, I RISE TO A POINT OF ORDER, - I DOUBT THE PRESENCE OF A QUORUM.

CALL FOR A DIVISION OF THE ASSEMBLY

PURPOSE: TO OBTAIN A MORE ACCURATE VOTE.

QUALIFICATIONS: NO SECOND
NOT DEBATABLE
NOT AMENDABLE
DEMAND MOTION TO COUNT A STANDING VOTE

(NO VOTE IS TAKEN ON WHETHER OR NOT TO TAKE THE DIVISION)

FORM: "I CALL FOR A DIVISION OF THE ASSEMBLY."

OH 8-3

DIVIDE THE QUESTION

PURPOSE: TO SEPARATE AN ITEM INTO TWO PARTS WHICH CAN STAND ALONE WITHOUT NEED OF THE OTHER PART.

QUALIFICATIONS: REQUIRES SECOND
AMENDABLE
NOT DEBATABLE
MAJORITY VOTE

FORM: "I MOVE WE DIVIDE THE QUESTION AND CONSIDER AS TWO PARTS, THE FIRST BEING . . . , AND THE THE SECOND . . ."

OBJECT TO THE CONSIDERATION OF THE QUESTION

PURPOSE: PREVENT AN ITEM OF BUSINESS FROM BEING FORMALLY CONSIDERED.

QUALIFICATIONS: REQUIRES NO SECOND
NOT DEBATABLE
NOT AMENDABLE
2/3 VOTE

- MUST BE MADE BEFORE ANY DISCUSSION HAS OCCURRED ON THE ORIGINAL MAIN MOTION.

SUSPEND THE RULES

PURPOSE: TO DO SOMETHING NOT POSSIBLE UNDER REGULAR STANDING RULES, SUSPENSION CANNOT CONFLICT WITH CONSTITUTION, BYLAWS, OR FUNDAMENTAL PARLIAMENTARY LAW.

QUALIFICATIONS: REQUIRES SECOND
NOT DEBATABLE
NOT AMENDABLE
2/3 VOTE

- MUST STATE PURPOSE OF SUSPENSION
- PARLIAMENTARIANS MUST INVESTIGATE SPECIAL CASES TO SUSPEND THE RULES.

CLOSE NOMINATIONS

PURPOSE: USUALLY DONE EITHER UNNECESSARILY OR ILLEGALLY IN SMALL SOCIETIES.
TO FORMALLY CLOSE NOMINATIONS.

QUALIFICATIONS: REQUIRES SECOND
NOT DEBATABLE
IS AMENDABLE
2/3 VOTE

OH 8-5

REOPEN NOMINATIONS

PURPOSE: TO ADD MORE NAMES TO THE BALLOT AFTER NOMINATIONS HAVE BEEN CLOSED OR PRIOR TO VOTING.

QUALIFICATIONS: REQUIRES SECOND
NOT DEBATABLE
IS AMENDABLE
MAJORITY VOTE

- MUST BE DONE BEFORE VOTING STARTS.

CHOOSE A METHOD OF VOTING

PURPOSE: DETERMINE ANOTHER METHOD OF VOTING OTHER THAN "VIVA VOICE" OR STANDING.

QUALIFICATIONS: REQUIRES SECOND
NOT DEBATABLE
IS AMENDABLE
MAJORITY VOTE

OH 8-6

APPEAL FROM THE DECISION OF THE CHAIR

PURPOSE: MEANS BY WHICH TO DISAGREE WITH DECISION OF THE CHAIR.

QUALIFICATIONS: REQUIRES SECOND
DEBATABLE - UNLESS ORIGINAL MOTION IS UNDEBATABLE
NOT AMENDABLE
MAJORITY VOTE

- APPEAL MUST TAKE PLACE IMMEDIATELY AFTER RULING OR BEFORE OTHER BUSINESS IS BROUGHT TO THE FLOOR.

LESSON 9

COURSE:

UNIT: Leadership

PROBLEM AREA: Parliamentary Procedure - (Restoratory motions)

PROBLEM: What is a basic description of restoratory (unclassified) motions in general and specifically the motions; to take from the table, to reconsider, to rescind, and to ratify.

OUTCOMES:
1. To describe the group of motions called unclassified or restoratory.
2. To list the restoratory motions with the essential descriptive characteristics of each.
3. To describe in detail the motion to take from the table.
4. To describe in detail the motion to reconsider.
5. To describe in detail the motion to rescind.
6. To describe in detail the motion to ratify.

REFERENCE: Robert's Rules of Order

Key Question #1

What is a general description of the group of motions known as "unclassified"?

The motions are very complex and have so many variations with different situations that it would be difficult to give a general description. It may suffice to say that parliamentary law prevents a society from having to decide the same, or basically the same, question during the same or subsequent sessions. Therefore, rules called renewal or restoration motions are available so that when correctly used, they can properly bring a question to the floor again.

Key Question #2

List the unclassified motions and the essential descriptive characteristics of each.

Restoratory Motions (Unclassified)

Motion	Second Required	Debatable	Amend.	Vote Req.	Purpose
Take from the table	yes	no	no	M	Bring a tabled question before assembly again
Reconsider	yes	yes/no	no	M	Revote on a previous motion
Rescind	yes	yes	yes	2/3	Cancel a motion before an action is taken
Ratify, approve, confirm	yes	yes	yes	M	Legalize action done without previous authority

Key Question #3

What is the purpose of the motion to take from the table?

> Its purpose is to take a motion which was previously laid on the table, from the table. It is not in order unless business has been transacted between the time it was laid on the table and the time it was taken from the table.

Key Question #4

What are the essential descriptive characteristics of the motion to take from the table?

> In order to take a motion from the table a second is required, there can be no debate or amendments, and it requires a majority vote.

Key Question #5

What form is used to state the motion to take from the table?

> Member: **"I move to take the motion, to buy a flag, from the table."**

Key Question #6

What is the purpose of the motion to reconsider?

> Its purpose is to bring an item of business back before the group to be voted on again. It is used when one thinks the decision of the group may be changed.

Key Question #7

What are the essential descriptive characteristics of the motion to reconsider?

> In order to make the motion to reconsider a member you must have voted on the prevailing side, and she may make the motion on the same day immediately following the first voting or at the next regular session only. After the next session, the motions to reconsider is no longer considerable.
>
> The motion to reconsider requires a second, is debatable if the motion to be reconsidered is debatable, it is not amendable, and requires a majority vote.

Key Question #8

What form is used to state the motion to reconsider?

> Member: **"Having voted on the prevailing side, I move to reconsider the motion which passed at our last meeting which stated that 'we buy a flag'."**

Key Question #9

What is the purpose of the motion to rescind?

> Here the purpose of the motion is to void a previous motion. This can be used when it is too late to reconsider or, in some instances, where it is desirable to strike a motion from the minutes.

Key Question #10

What are the essential descriptive characteristics of the motion to rescind?

> A second is required on this motion, it is amendable and debatable, and usually requires a two-thirds vote.

Key Question #11

What form is used to state the motion to rescind?

> Member: **"Before any action is taken, I move to rescind the motion which passed at our regular meeting two months ago which stated that 'we buy a flag'."**

Key Question #12

What is the purpose of the motion to ratify?

> The motion to ratify is a main motion, and is the means by which the group makes valid the action of some committee's emergency action, action taken by the executive board, or business transacted without the presence of a quorum.

Key Question #13

What are the essential descriptive characteristics of the motion to ratify?

> The motion to ratify, since it is a main motion, has the same qualifications as a main motion; therefore, it requires a second, is amendable and debatable and requires a majority vote.

Key Question #14

What form is used in stating the motion to ratify?

> Member: **"I move that our organization ratify the action taken by the executive committee to buy a new flag for the meeting room."**

UNCLASSIFIED MOTIONS (RESTORATORY

TAKE FROM THE TABLE

TO MOVE TO RECONSIDER

TO RESCIND

TO RATIFY

TAKE FROM THE TABLE

PURPOSE: TO TAKE A MOTION PREVIOUSLY LAID ON THE TABLE, FROM THE TABLE.
NOT IN ORDER UNLESS BUSINESS HAS BEEN TRANSACTED BETWEEN TIME IT WAS LAID ON TABLE AND TAKEN FROM TABLE. (CHANGE OF PARLIAMENTARY LEVEL.)

QUALIFICATIONS: SECOND

NOT AMENDABLE

NOT DEBATABLE

MAJORITY VOTE

TO RECONSIDER

PURPOSE: BRING AN ITEM BACK BEFORE THE GROUP

QUALIFICATIONS: SECOND

DEBATABLE IF MOTION BEING RECONSIDERED IS DEBATABLE

NOT DEBATABLE

MAJORITY VOTE

- MUST HAVE VOTED ON PREVAILING SIDE

- MUST OCCUR ON SAME DAY OR NEXT REGULAR MEETING

OH 9-3

RESCIND

PURPOSE: VOID A PREVIOUS MOTION, MAY BE USED WHEN TOO LATE TO RECONSIDER

QUALIFICATIONS: SECOND
AMENDABLE
DEBATABLE
2/3 VOTE

RATIFY

PURPOSE: MAKE VALID THE ACTION OF ANY COMMITTEE, OR A SOCIETY IF BUSINESS WAS TRANSACTED WITHOUT A QUORUM

QUALIFICATIONS: SECOND
AMENDABLE
DEBATABLE
MAJORITY VOTE

- IS A MAIN MOTION

Parliamentary Procedure At a Glance

The first 13 motions below are listed in established order of precedence. When one is pending, you may not introduce another that is listed below it, but you may introduce another that is above it. There is no order of precedence among the remaining 10 motions.

	Type of Motion	Interrupt Speaker	Require Second	Amendable	Debatable	Required Vote	Purpose	Page
1. Fix the Time to Which To Adjourn	Privileged	No	Yes	Yes	Yes	Majority	to set time for next meeting	34
2. Adjourn	Privileged	No	Yes	No	No	Majority	to close the meeting	33
3. Take a Recess	Privileged	No	Yes	Yes	No	Majority	to interrupt the meeting (intermission)	33
4. Raise a Question of Privilege	Privileged	Yes	No	No	No	- -	to request immediate action	32
5. Call for the Orders of the Day	Privileged	Yes	No	No	No	- -	to require adherence to agenda	31
6. Lay on the Table	Subsidiary	No	Yes	No	No	Majority	to temporarily interrupt business	25
7. Prev. Question (Close Debate)	Subsidiary	No	Yes	No	No	2/3	to close debate on pending motion	24
8. Limit or Extend Limits of Debate	Subsidiary	No	Yes	Yes	No	2/3	to limit or extend debate	23
9. Postpone to a Certain Time (Postpone Definitely)	Subsidiary	No	Yes	Yes	Yes	Majority	to postpone to another, specified time (delay action)	22
10. Refer to Committee	Subsidiary	No	Yes	Yes	Yes	Majority	to send to a committee for further study	19
11. Amend	Subsidiary	No	Yes	Yes	Yes	Majority	to alter or modify the wording of a motion or resolution	18
12. Postpone Indefinitely	Subsidiary	No	Yes	No	Yes	Majority	to avoid a direct vote on a motion	13
13. Original Main Motion (Resolution)	Main	No	Yes	Yes	Yes	Majority	to introduce new business	7
14. Point of Order	Incidental	Yes	No	No	No	- -	to enforce rules and orders	47
15. Appeal	Incidental	Yes	Yes	No	Yes	Majority	try to reverse ruling of the chair	53
16. Questions or Points of Information	Incidental	Yes	No	No	No	- -	obtain answers to questions and seek information	40
17. Suspend the Rules	Incidental	No	Yes	No	No	2/3	set aside rules that interfere with action desired	50
18. Object to Consideration	Incidental	Yes	No	No	No	2/3	to suppress action	50
19. Division of a Question	Incidental	No	Yes	Yes	No	Majority	to divide a question	49
20. Division of the Assembly	Incidental	Yes	No	No	No	- -	to provide for a more accurate count of the vote	48
21. Take From the Table	Bring Back Before Assembly	No	Yes	No	No	Majority	to bring a tabled question before assembly again	61
22. Rescind	Bring Back Before Assembly	No	Yes	Yes	Yes	2/3	to nullify a motion previously adopted before action is taken	62
23. Reconsider	Bring Back Before Assembly	Yes	Yes	No	Yes	Majority	to bring back for review	62

A MOTION TO CLOSE NOMINATIONS IS OUT OF ORDER. THE CHAIR SHOULD CALL FOR FURTHER NOMINATIONS THREE (3) TIMES. UPON HEARING NO FURTHER NOMINATIONS, THE NOMINATIONS MAY BE CLOSED BY THE CHAIR'S DECLARATION. (pp. 5

www.ingramcontent.com/pod-product-compliance
Lightning Source LLC
LaVergne TN
LVHW080442210426
836850LV00037B/828